Published By Robert Corbin

@ Jose Price

The Alkaline Diet: the Elegant Recipes for Weight

Loss

All Right RESERVED

ISBN 978-87-94477-86-4

TABLE OF CONTENTS

French Toast 1

Apple Pancakes 3

Avocado Salad For Breakfast... 4

Quinoa Salad With Alkaline Veggies 7

Lentil Soup.. 9

Omelet With Mushrooms And Spinach.......................... 12

Salad With Lentils And Quinoa 14

Vegetable Soup 15

Quinoa Salad With Roasted Vegetables......................... 18

Kale And Avocado Salad With Lemon Dressing............. 21

Mint & Lemongrass Vitamin Water................................ 24

Ultimate Citrus Vitamin Water.. 26

Very Berry Vitamin Water 27

Tofu Scramble 29

Coconut Chia Seed Pudding 31

Fruit Salad... 32

Sesame Dressing And Noodles.. 33

4 Oz Roasted Salmon, ½ Baked Potato, Curried Beets And Vegetables 36

Turmeric Roasted Cauliflower And Kale 38

Summer Salad With Mint And Lemon Dressing 41

Lime And Coconut Panna Cotta 44

Broccoli Mushroom Rotini Casserole 46

Alkaline Oat 49

Mix The Sprout Salad 52

Kale Chickpea Mash 54

Quinoa And Apple Breakfast 56

Almond-Crusted Tofu With Alkaline Quinoa 57

Stuffed Portobello Mushrooms 60

Brown Rice Alkaline Veggie Stir-Fry 63

Hummus With Carrot Sticks 65

Cucumber And Mint Gazpacho 67

Watermelon And Feta Salad With Balsamic Glaze 70

Broccoli Soup 72

Baked Avocado And Egg 75

Overnight Oats 77

Veggie Scramble 79

Oatmeal And Almond Butter... 81

Bowl With Vegetables 82

Zucchini Noodles And Kale Pesto 85

Crunchy Kale Salad With Tahini Dressing 87

Raw Pad Thai With Zucchini Noodles 89

Chickpea Quinoa Vegetable Bowl 92

Cannellini Bean & Artichoke Spread 95

Hearty Vegetable Soup.. 97

Sesame Tahini Dressing 101

Cucumber-Mint Infused Water 102

Green Detox Smoothie 103

Yummy Cold Oats 105

Scrambled Tofu 106

Thewlis 108

Guacamole With Veggie Sticks 110

Arugula, Beetroot, And Walnut Salad 112

Cauliflower And Coconut Curry Soup	114
Quinoa Salad	117
Almond Butter And Banana Toast	120
Acai Bowl	122
Chickpea Omelets	124
Energy Shake	127
Quinoa Burrito Bowl	128
Wild Rice Mushrooms And Almond Risotto	130
Eggplant Chickpea Stew	132
Cucumber & Tomatillo Breakfast Shake	134
Black Bean & Tomato Soup	136
Raw Chocolate Pudding	138
Maple Millet Porridge	140
Chickpea Fritatta	142
Alkaline Berry Crumble	144

French Toast

Ingredients:

- 1 teaspoon of cinnamon powder
- 1 teaspoon salt, to taste
- 1 teaspoon vanilla extract
- 6 slices of brown bread
- 2 eggs
- 1/2 cup of milk
- 1/4 teaspoon nutmeg

Directions:

1. In a bowl, whisk together the eggs, milk, salt, spices, and vanilla.
2. After dipping the bread into the egg mixture, let it soak on both sides.

3. Pour oil into a pan and heat it over a low flame.
4. Toast the bread until both sides are golden brown.
5. Serve warm with a dollop of butter.

Apple Pancakes

Ingredients:

- 2 red apples, grated
- 2 teaspoons vegetable oil
- 1 peeled kiwifruit
- A hand full of blueberries
- 1/2 cup of low-fat frozen yogurt
- 1/2 cup of flour
- 1/2 teaspoon of cinnamon powder
- 1 egg beaten
- 1/3 of a cup of milk
- One handful of granola

Directions:

1. In a bowl, mix together flour and cinnamon. Pour in some milk and eggs. Continue whisking until the mixture becomes smooth.
2. Add oil to a pan before heating it. Reduce the heat.
3. Pour the apple mixture into the pan.
4. Spread the Ingredients: out and simmer for two minutes.
5. Divide them into different batches.
6. Serve with kiwi, yogurt, blueberries, and granola.

Avocado Salad for Breakfast

Ingredients:

- 1 pink grapefruit

- Just a few almonds

- 4 handfuls of spinach
- 2 teaspoons chili sauce
- 3 tomatoes
- 1/2 red onions
- 1 tortilla
- 1/2 pack of firm tofu
- 1 avocado
- 1/2 lemon

Directions:

1. The tortillas should be heated in an oven.
2. After you've heated them, bake them for 8 to 10 minutes.
3. On one side, chop some tofu, onions, and tomatoes.
4. Combine with chili sauce.
5. Refrigerate for some time.

6. Almonds, grapefruit, and avocados should be chopped also.
7. Mix them all together and spread them evenly over the bowl.
8. Add some freshly squeezed lemon juice!

Quinoa Salad with Alkaline Veggies

Ingredients:

- 1/4 cup coarsely chopped red onion

- 1/8 cup freshly minced lemon juice - 1/4 cup fresh parsley

- -2 tsp. extra virgin olive oil

- 1 cup quinoa, 2 cups water, 1 diced cucumber, 1 diced bell pepper, and 1 shredded carrot.

- 1 cup halved cherry tomatoes

- To taste, salt and pepper

Directions:

1. Rinse the quinoa thoroughly under cold water.
2. Heat the water to a rolling boil in a medium saucepan.

3. Stir in the quinoa, lower the heat to a simmer, cover the pot, and cook for about 15 minutes, or until the water is completely absorbed.
4. Take it off the heat, cover it, and let it stand for five minutes. Fluff with a fork, then place aside to cool.
5. Combine the chopped cucumber, bell pepper, carrot, cherry tomatoes, red onion, and parsley in a sizable bowl.
6. Stir the chilled quinoa into the mixture.
7. Combine the lemon juice, olive oil, salt, and pepper in a small bowl.
8. After adding the dressing, mix the quinoa salad to evenly distribute it.
9. Taste and, if necessary, adjust seasoning.
10. Either serve right away or chill for a few hours to let the flavors meld.
11. Enjoy as a side dish with your preferred protein or as a light meal.

Lentil Soup

Ingredients:

- 2 chopped celery stalks
- 1 diced zucchini
- 1 chopped red bell pepper
- 1 cup washed green lentils
- 1 chopped onion - 3 minced garlic cloves - 2 peeled and sliced carrots
- 4 cups of vegetable broth, 2 teaspoons of tomato paste, 1 teaspoon each of turmeric, cumin, paprika, dried thyme, salt to taste, and fresh parsley for garnish.

Directions:

1. Heat some water in a big saucepan over medium heat.

2. Sauté the onions and minced garlic until they are fragrant and translucent.
3. Include the chopped red bell pepper, carrots, celery, and zucchini and sauté for an additional 2 to 3 minutes, or until the veggies start to soften.
4. Add the tomato paste, vegetable broth, and washed green lentils.
5. Fill the saucepan with the dried thyme, turmeric, cumin, and paprika. Stir well to completely combine all the Ingredients:.
6. After the soup comes to a boil, turn down the heat. When the lentils are done, cover the pot and boil it for 30 to 40 minutes.
7. Season the soup with a pinch of salt and pepper.
8. Dish up the soup and top each bowl with a sprig of fresh parsley.

9. Enjoy this hearty, alkaline lentil soup with the knowledge that you are supplying your body with healthy nutrients.
10. For a complete and balanced alkaline dinner, serve it with a side salad or as a cozy stand-alone dish. For a lively and healthy lifestyle, be sure to try more of our cookbook's alkaline recipes.

Omelet with Mushrooms and Spinach

Ingredients:

- ½ cup diced mushrooms

- ¼ teaspoon sea salt

- ¼ cup chopped onion

- 1 tablespoon of olive oil

Directions:

1. In a big skillet, warm up over medium heat. should be added. While intermittently stirring, cook for 5 minutes.
2. Four eggs and ¼ cup water are whisked together.
3. Cook the egg mixture in the skillet for one minute after adding it. 1 cup of spinach leaves should be added.

4. Stir for 2 minutes. After one minute of cooking, flip the omelet.

Salad with Lentils and Quinoa

Ingredients:

- ¼ cup diced cucumber
- ¼ cup minced parsley
- 1 tablespoon olive oil
- 1 tablespoon lemon juice
- ½ cup of quinoa
- ½ cup of lentils
- ½ cup diced tomatoes
- ¼ cup diced red onion

Directions:

1. Prepare and cook quinoa and lentils then combined them all in a big bowl.

Vegetable Soup

Ingredients:

- 2 celery stalks, sliced
- 1 bell pepper, diced
- 2 zucchini, diced
- 1 cup broccoli florets
- 1 cup cauliflower florets
- 4 cups vegetable broth
- 1 teaspoon dried thyme
- 1 teaspoon dried oregano
- 1 tablespoon olive oil
- 1 onion, diced
- 2 cloves garlic, minced

- 2 carrots, sliced

- Salt and pepper to taste

- Fresh parsley, chopped (for garnish)

Directions:
1. In a large pot, heat the olive oil over medium heat.
2. Add the diced onion and minced garlic to the pot and sauté until the onion becomes translucent and fragrant.
3. Add the sliced carrots, celery, bell pepper, zucchini, broccoli florets, and cauliflower florets to the pot. Stir well to combine.
4. Pour in the vegetable broth and bring the mixture to a boil.
5. Reduce the heat to a simmer and add the dried thyme and oregano. Season with salt and pepper to taste.

6. Cover the pot and let the soup simmer for about 20-25 minutes, or until the vegetables are tender.
7. Once the vegetables are cooked to your desired consistency, remove the pot from heat.
8. Using an immersion blender or a countertop blender, carefully blend the soup until it reaches your desired consistency. Be cautious when blending hot liquids.
9. Return the blended soup to the pot and heat it over low heat for a few minutes to ensure it's warm.
10. Adjust the seasoning if needed.
11. Ladle the Alkaline Vegetable Soup into bowls and garnish with freshly chopped parsley.
12. Serve the soup immediately and enjoy the comforting flavors and alkaline goodness.

Quinoa Salad with Roasted Vegetables

Ingredients:

- 2 tablespoons olive oil

- 1 teaspoon dried herbs (such as thyme, rosemary, or oregano)

- Salt and pepper to taste

- 1/4 cup fresh herbs (such as parsley, basil, or cilantro), chopped

- Juice of 1 lemon

- 1 cup quinoa

- 2 cups water or vegetable broth

- 2 cups mixed vegetables (such as bell peppers, zucchini, cherry tomatoes, and red onion), diced

- Optional toppings: crumbled feta cheese, toasted nuts (such as almonds or walnuts)

Directions:

1. Preheat your oven to 400°F (200°C).
2. Rinse the quinoa thoroughly under cold water to remove any bitterness.
3. In a saucepan, combine the rinsed quinoa and water or vegetable broth. Bring to a boil over medium heat.
4. Reduce the heat to low, cover, and simmer for about 15-20 minutes, or until the quinoa is cooked and the liquid is absorbed. Fluff the quinoa with a fork and set aside.
5. While the quinoa is cooking, prepare the roasted vegetables. In a baking dish, toss the diced vegetables with olive oil, dried herbs, salt, and pepper until evenly coated.
6. Spread the vegetables in a single layer on the baking dish and roast in the preheated oven

for about 20-25 minutes, or until they are tender and slightly caramelized.

7. Once the roasted vegetables are ready, remove them from the oven and let them cool slightly.
8. In a large bowl, combine the cooked quinoa, roasted vegetables, fresh herbs, and lemon juice. Toss gently to combine.
9. Season with additional salt and pepper if needed.
10. If desired, sprinkle crumbled feta cheese and toasted nuts on top of the salad for added flavor and texture.
11. Serve the Quinoa Salad with Roasted Vegetables at room temperature or chilled, and enjoy the vibrant and wholesome flavors.

Kale and Avocado Salad with Lemon Dressing

Ingredients:

- 1/2 cup cherry tomatoes, halved

- 1/4 cup red onion, thinly sliced

- 2 tablespoons chopped fresh cilantro or parsley

- Juice of 1 lemon

- 2 tablespoons extra-virgin olive oil

- 4 cups chopped kale leaves

- 1 ripe avocado, pitted and diced

- Salt and pepper to taste

- Optional toppings: crumbled feta cheese, toasted sunflower seeds, or chopped almonds

Directions:

1. In a large bowl, add the chopped kale leaves.
2. Massage the kale leaves gently with your hands for a few minutes to help soften them and reduce bitterness.
3. Add the diced avocado, cherry tomatoes, red onion, and chopped cilantro or parsley to the bowl. Toss gently to combine.
4. In a separate small bowl, whisk together the lemon juice, olive oil, salt, and pepper to make the dressing.
5. Pour the lemon dressing over the kale and avocado mixture. Toss well to evenly coat the salad.
6. Let the salad sit for about 10-15 minutes to allow the flavors to meld together and the kale to absorb the dressing.
7. If desired, sprinkle crumbled feta cheese, toasted sunflower seeds, or chopped almonds

on top of the salad for added texture and flavor.
8. Serve the Kale and Avocado Salad with Lemon Dressing as a refreshing side dish or a light lunch.

Mint & Lemongrass Vitamin Water

Ingredients:

- Juice of ½ lemon
- 1 cup pineapple
- Small handful fresh mint (to taste)
- 1 inch fresh lemongrass
- 1 liter filtered water
- 3 inches fresh ginger

Directions:
1. Place ginger and mint in a small bowl and muddle (crush gently) with the back of a spoon or with a muddler.
2. Next add the pineapple chunks and repeat the process.

3. Then throw all of the ingredients into a large glass jar or stainless steel bottle and top up with the water.
4. Place into your fridge for 4-8 hours to infuse, then enjoy!

Ultimate Citrus Vitamin Water

Ingredients:

- Juice of ½ lemon
- 1 liter filtered water
- 1 medium grapefruit
- ½ lemon, thinly sliced
- ½ lime, thinly sliced
- 1 orange, thinly sliced

Directions:
1. Juice the grapefruit and lemon, and add to a large glass jar or stainless steel bottle.
2. Add the slices of citrus fruit and top up with the filtered water.
3. Replace the lid and leave to sit and infuse in the fridge for 4-8 hours.

Very Berry Vitamin Water

Ingredients:

- 1 liter filtered water

- Juice of ½ lemon

- 1 cup fresh coconut water

- 1/2 cup blackberries

- 1 teaspoon spirulina powder

- 1/2 cup raspberries

Directions:

1. Place the berries into a small bowl and pour over some of the coconut water. Muddle (gently crush).
2. Add the rest of the ingredients, taking care to stir the spirulina powder into the water well.

3. Top up with filtered water, pour into a glass jar or bottle, and leave to sit in the fridge for 4-8 hours.

Tofu Scramble

Ingredients:

- 1/2 teaspoon garlic powder
- 1/2 cup diced bell peppers (any color)
- 1/2 cup diced tomatoes
- Handful of spinach
- Salt and pepper to taste
- 1/2 block of tofu, crumbled
- 1 tablespoon nutritional yeast
- 1/2 teaspoon turmeric
- 1 tablespoon olive oil

Directions:

1. Heat olive oil in a skillet over medium heat.

2. Add crumbled tofu, nutritional yeast, turmeric, garlic powder, salt, and pepper.
3. Sauté for 5 minutes, until tofu starts to brown slightly.
4. Add diced bell peppers and tomatoes to the skillet and cook for an additional 3 minutes.
5. Stir in spinach and cook until wilted.
6. Serve hot.

Coconut Chia Seed Pudding

Ingredients:

- 1 cup coconut milk
- 1 tablespoon maple syrup
- 1/4 cup chia seeds
- 1/4 teaspoon vanilla extract

Directions:

1. In a bowl, combine chia seeds, coconut milk, maple syrup, and vanilla extract.
2. Stir well until all Ingredients: are evenly distributed.
3. Refrigerate for at least 2 hours or overnight.
4. Serve chilled.

Fruit Salad

Ingredients:

- 2 oranges, peeled and segmented
- 1 cup grapes
- 1 cup pineapple chunks
- 1 cup mixed berries (such as strawberries, blueberries, and blackberries)
- 2 apples, cubed
- Fresh mint leaves for garnish

Directions:
1. In a large bowl, combine all the fruits.
2. Toss gently to mix.
3. Garnish with fresh mint leaves.
4. Serve chilled.

Sesame Dressing And Noodles

INGREDIENTS:

For the salad:

- 3 peppers, cut into small, thin pieces

- 400 grams chicken breast without skin without bone

- ½ cup of cashews or peanuts

- 1 cup chopped cilantro leaves

- 4 green onions or green onions, only green parts, chopped

- 5-6 cups kale or spinach

- 1/2 cup of brown rice noodles

- 3 large carrots, cut into small, thin pieces

For the dressing:

- 2 tablespoons of honey

- 1 tablespoon ginger, chopped

- some squeezes of lemon juice

- 2 large cloves of garlic, peeled

- ¼ cup of natural peanut butter

- ⅓ cup of soy sauce

- ¼ cup white distilled vinegar

- ½ cup of coconut oil

- 2 tablespoons of water

- 2 tablespoons of sesame oil

DIRECTIONS:

1. In a bowl of cold water, soak the noodles. Preheat the oven to 200 ° C. In a food

processor, mix the ingredients of the dressing, pushing away the peanut butter.
2. To marinate, add the chicken in a plastic bag and add ¼ to ½ cup of the dressing for approximately 15-30 minutes. In the food processor, add the peanut butter and press.
3. Mix all the vegetables in a bowl. Bake the marinated chicken for 20 minutes, set aside for 10 minutes and then pour the vegetable mixture.
4. Then, drain the noodles and cook them in a skillet over medium-high heat. Add a little oil, a little of the dressing, and stir while it is soft. Add a little water if necessary. At the end, garnish with crushed cilantro and peanuts.

4 Oz Roasted Salmon, ½ Baked Potato, Curried Beets And Vegetables

INGREDIENTS:

- 1/2 teaspoon chili powder
- 1/2 serrano chili
- 1/4 semolina
- 1 cup of water
- 1/2 teaspoon ground cumin
- 1 tablespoon of lemon juice
- 1 bunch of beet / beet leaves
- 1/2 small onion, finely chopped
- 1/4 cup stems, finely chopped
- 1 tablespoon of coconut oil

- 3 garlic cloves

- 1/2 teaspoon of turmeric

- pinch of salt (or to taste)

DIRECTIONS:

1. At medium heat, heat the oil in a pan and add the stems of beet, garlic, chili and onion.
2. Cook them until the onions become transparent. Then, add the semolina and cook for 3 minutes.
3. Add the cumin, chili powder and turmeric, and then the beets, salt and water. Cover the pan and cook for 5 minutes.
4. Cook for 5 more with the pan uncovered, and stir frequently. At the end, sprinkle with lemon juice.

Turmeric Roasted Cauliflower and Kale

Ingredients:

- Cayenne pepper, .25 teaspoon

- Turmeric, ground, one tablespoon

- Tomatoes, organic, two

- Avocado, organic, one half

- Celery, organic, one stalk

- Green bell pepper, organic, one

- Kale, organic, three cups washed and rinsed

- Cauliflower, organic, one half of one head washed and rinsed

- Olive oil, two tablespoons

- Coconut oil, two tablespoons

- Pumpkin seed, organic, .5 cup

- Sea salt, one teaspoon

- Black pepper, one teaspoon

- Tamari, organic, .25 teaspoon

- Lemon juice, two tablespoons

- Paprika, .25 teaspoon

Directions:

1. Heat the oven to 350. Chop the cauliflower in to small florets. Put them in a mixing bowl and mix with the salt, pepper, paprika, cayenne pepper, turmeric, and the coconut oil and mix well.
2. Arrange the cauliflower on a cookie sheet and bake for twenty minutes. While the cauliflower is baking chop the kale into bite size pieces.

3. Mix the kale with the tamari and the lemon juice and place on serving plates. Slice very thin the celery and bell pepper and lay the slices on top of the kale.
4. Chop the tomatoes and the avocado and sprinkle these pieces over the vegetable slices.
5. Add on the pumpkin seeds and pour a thin stream of olive oil over all. Lay the baked cauliflower over all and serve.

Summer Salad with Mint and Lemon Dressing

Ingredients:

SALAD

- Parsley, organic, .5 cup chopped
- Cilantro, organic, .5 cup chopped
- Asparagus, organic, three bunches
- Avocado, organic, peeled and sliced
- Zucchini, organic, two thin sliced
- Green peas, organic, one cup cooked and cooled
- Radish, organic, five thin sliced

DRESSING

- Olive oil, organic, two tablespoons

- Garlic, organic, one clove minced

- Shallots, organic, two diced

- Sea salt, one teaspoon

- Black pepper, one teaspoon

- Dijon mustard, one tablespoon

- Lemon juice, organic, three tablespoons

Directions:

1. Blanch the asparagus and then slice it long wise to get long strips.
2. Fry the strips of zucchini until they are lightly brown. In a large bowl mix the peas, radishes, parsley, cilantro, avocado, zucchini, and asparagus. Blend all the dressing Ingredients: together until smooth.
3. Add the well mixed dressing to the salad and toss lightly.

4. To blanch the asparagus (or any fruit or vegetable) put the item into boiling water for one minute and then plunge it into a bowl of ice water.

LIME AND COCONUT PANNA COTTA

INGREDIENTS:

- 1/2 teaspoon lime extract

- 3 tablespoons or more agave nectar/ jaggery

- Lime zest

- Green food color (optional)

- 1/2 cup water

- 1/2 cup coconut milk

- 1/2 teaspoon agar agar powder

- Chopped pineapple or berries

DIRECTIONS:

1. Dissolve the agar agar powder with 1/4 cup water in a saucepan. Let it stand for about 5

minutes. Warm the coconut milk in another saucepan.
2. Put the saucepan with the dissolved agar agar over a low flame and stir continuously.
3. When it comes to a boil, add in the warm coconut milk, rest of the water, lime essence, sugar, zest and colour.
4. Stir till all the Ingredients:are incorporated. Taste it and add more sweetener if you desire.
5. After 3 or 4 minutes take it off the stove and put it into small bowls to set. This usually sets at room temperature, but tastes better when it is cold.
6. So let it set in the fridge for a while and serve cold with chopped pineapple, berries or some berry coulis if you like

BROCCOLI MUSHROOM ROTINI CASSEROLE

INGREDIENTS:

FOR THE CASSEROLE:

- 1/2 teaspoon dried oregano

- Paprika, to garnish

- White pepper, to garnish

- Herbamare or salt, to garnish

- 1 cup of broccoli

- 8 ounces sliced mushrooms

- 1 medium onion, peeled and quartered

- 3 large cloves of garlic

- 16 ounces whole wheat rotini, elbows or spirals

- 1/4 cup panko bread crumbs

- 1/2 teaspoon dried basil

FOR THE CHEESY SAUCE:

- 5 teaspoon brown rice miso paste

- 1 tablespoon cornstarch

- 1 teaspoon smoked paprika

- 2 cups almond milk

- 1/4 cup cashews

- 1 large clove of garlic

- 1/3 cup nutritional yeast

DIRECTIONS:

1. Preheat oven to 350 F.

2. Bring a large pot of water to a boil. Add salt if desired. Cook rotini or spirals for about 6 minutes just until al dente. (Do not overcook)
3. Pulse, broccoli, mushrooms, onions and garlic separately in a food processor (unless you have a very large one) until broken into tiny pieces. Add to a large wok or sauté pan and cook for 7 minutes until soft. Add a little water or vegetable broth as necessary to cook.
4. Blend cheezy sauce Ingredients:in a blender and taste test. Adjust seasonings if desired with more salt and pepper or smoked paprika.
5. Drain rotini and add to sauté pan and pour sauce over (or combine in a large pot if you don't have a lot of room). Toss to coat.
6. Pour into a large casserole pan. Top with panko breadcrumbs and smoked paprika.
7. Bake for 20-25 minutes.Serve and enjoy!

ALKALINE OAT

Ingredients:

- Coconut oil (1 dessert spoon per person)

- Water

- Nut Milk

- Coconut/non-dairy yoghurt

- Cinnamon (1 tsp per person)

- Handful of mixed nuts/seeds

- Oats (preferably organic)

- Chia seeds (1 dessert spoon per person)

- Optional: berries of your choice

Directions:

1. Basically cook your regular amount of oats in WATER. Not milk. WATER.
2. So add the oats and water to a pan and bring to a simmer and then add the chia seeds. Cook until it's a touch too dry for your liking and then stir in a splash or two of the nut milk (I love coconut milk, but any other non-dairy milk is fine).
3. Remove from the heat and then stir in the coconut oil, cinnamon and a dollop of the non-dairy yoghurt.
4. Top with the nuts and seeds and then finish with blueberries or strawberries if this is part of your fruit for the day (I recommend keeping your fructose intake down so 1-2 serves of in-season fruit per day).
5. Just swapping the 250ml of milk per person, taking out the sugar/honey, and adding in chia (omega 3 and extra fibre to support digestion, brain function, metabolism, heart health),

coconut oil (MCT oils for metabolism, lowering bad cholesterol and brain function) and cinnamon (speeded metabolism, lower blood sugar levels, reduce heart disease risk factors) – you're turning a 'regular' breakfast into a SUPER ALKALINE BREAKFAST.
6. It rocks and is a saviour for me on many-a-busy-morning getting myself and the family ready for work/school/kindy!

Mix The Sprout Salad

Ingredients:

- 1/2 cup of baby spinach or arugula
- 2 tablespoons of olive oil
- 1/2 teaspoon of the Italian herb mix
- 1/2 cup lime juice
- 1/2 cup fenugreek sprouts
- 1/2 cup radicchio or red cabbage
- 1 small radish, cut thinly
- Season with salt to taste.
- Ground black pepper, just a pinch

Directions:

1. Toss the vegetables and sprouts together in a large bowl.
2. In a small bowl, combine olive oil, Italian herb mix, lime juice, salt, and black pepper.
3. Pour the salad dressing over the vegetables and stir them together.

Kale Chickpea Mash

Ingredients:

- A bunch of kale
- 1/2 cups boiled chickpeas
- 2 teaspoons of coconut oil
- 3 teaspoons of garlic
- 1 shallot (white onion)
- Celtic sea salt for taste

Directions:

1. Chop and then fry the shallot. Mix minced garlic with olive oil.
2. Allow it to turn golden brown before adding the greens, onion, and garlic.

3. After adding the chickpeas, cook for 6 minutes.
4. Mix in the remaining Ingredients:. Your meal is now prepared.

Quinoa and Apple Breakfast

Ingredients:

- 1/2 cup quinoa

- 1 apple

- 1/2 lemon

- Pinch of cinnamon

Directions:

1. Cook the quinoa in accordance with the Directions: on the back of the packet.
2. Add some liquid. Allow it to simmer and boil for fifteen minutes.
3. Add the grated apple to the quinoa and simmer for an additional 30 seconds.
4. Serve in a bowl. Sprinkle cinnamon on top. You may also include raisins if you so choose.

Almond-Crusted Tofu with Alkaline Quinoa

Ingredients:

- 1 cup of vegetable broth - 1/2 cup of quinoa - 1 tablespoon each of olive oil and soy sauce

- 1 teaspoon dried thyme, 1 tablespoon nutritional yeast, and 1/2 teaspoon garlic powder

- 1 cup of almond meal and 1 block of firm tofu

- -Garnish with fresh parsley- Season with salt and pepper to taste.

Directions:
1. Set the oven's temperature to 400°F (200°C). Use parchment paper to cover a baking sheet.
2. After thoroughly draining, rinse the quinoa with cold water.

3. Bring the vegetable broth to a boil in a saucepan. For about 15 minutes, or until the quinoa is cooked and the liquid has been absorbed, add the quinoa, lower the heat to low, cover, and simmer.
4. Drain and squeeze the tofu to get rid of extra moisture while you wait. Slice the tofu into large pieces.
5. Mix the almond meal, nutritional yeast, dried thyme, garlic powder, salt, and pepper in a shallow bowl.
6. After lightly pressing the tofu slices in the almond mixture to apply the coating, brush them with olive oil.
7. Spread the coated tofu slices out on the baking sheet that has been prepared, and bake for 20 to 25 minutes, or until the tofu is crispy and browned.
8. Use a fork to fluff the cooked quinoa and set it aside while the tofu bakes.

9. Combine the soy sauce, olive oil, and a dash of salt in a small bowl.
10. Remove the baked tofu from the oven and allow it to cool slightly.
11. Combine the cooked quinoa and the soy sauce mixture in a big bowl. Mix thoroughly by tossing.
12. Arrange the slices of almond-crusted tofu over a bed of alkaline quinoa. Add fresh parsley as a garnish.
13. Enjoy your quinoa with alkaline tofu and almond crust!

Stuffed Portobello Mushrooms

Ingredients:

- 1 cup sliced zucchini - 1 cup quartered cherry tomatoes
- Nutritional yeast, 1/4 cup
- 1 tablespoon soy sauce or tamari
- 1 teaspoon each of dried basil and oregano
- 4 large Portobello mushrooms - 1 tablespoon of olive oil - 1 cup of chopped spinach - 1 finely chopped onion
- To taste, add salt and pepper - Garnish with fresh parsley

Directions:
1. Set the oven temperature to 375°F (190°C). Remove the stems from the portobello

mushrooms and clean them. On a baking sheet covered with parchment paper, arrange them..

2. Over medium heat, warm the olive oil in a sizable skillet. Sauté the onion and garlic after being added until they are aromatic and transparent.

3. Include the zucchini, cherry tomatoes, and spinach in the skillet. The vegetables should be sautéed for a few minutes to gently cook them while keeping their crispness.

4. Turn off the heat and add the nutritional yeast, tamari or soy sauce, dried oregano, basil, salt, and pepper. Mix thoroughly to incorporate all flavors.

5. Generously fill each mushroom cap with the vegetable mixture before spooning it onto the Portobello mushrooms.

6. After the oven has been prepared, add the packed mushrooms and bake for 20 to 25

minutes, or until the mushrooms are soft and just beginning to brown.
7. Take the dish out of the oven and top with fresh parsley. Enjoy as a main course or side dish after serving hot.

Brown Rice Alkaline Veggie Stir-Fry

Ingredients:

- 1 cup mushrooms, sliced
- 2 minced garlic cloves
- 1 teaspoon grated ginger
- 1/4 cup soy sauce (low sodium)
- 1/4 teaspoon sea salt
- 14 teaspoon black pepper
- 2 cups brown rice, cooked
- 1 tablespoon coconut oil
- 1 sliced red bell pepper
- 1 sliced yellow bell pepper
- 1 pound snow peas

- 1 cup florets broccoli

Directions:

1. Heat the coconut oil in a big wok or skillet over medium-high heat.
2. To the skillet, add red and yellow bell peppers, snow peas, broccoli, mushrooms, garlic, and ginger.
3. Stir-fry the vegetables for 5-7 minutes, or until tender-crisp.
4. Pour in the cooked brown rice and stir to incorporate.
5. Stir-fry the rice and vegetables for another 2-3 minutes with low-sodium soy sauce.
6. Season with black pepper and sea salt.
7. Serve immediately.

Hummus with Carrot Sticks

Ingredients:

- 2 minced garlic cloves
- 1 tablespoon lemon juice
- 1/4 teaspoon sea salt
- 14 teaspoon black pepper
- 1 can drained and rinsed chickpeas
- 1 tbsp tahini
- 2 tablespoons olive oil
- Dupable carrot sticks

Directions:

1. Combine chickpeas, tahini, olive oil, garlic, lemon juice, sea salt, and black pepper in a food processor.

2. Blend until the mixture is smooth and creamy.
3. With carrot sticks for dipping, serve.

Cucumber and Mint Gazpacho

Ingredients:

- 1/4 cup fresh parsley leaves
- 1 small shallot, minced
- 2 cloves garlic, minced
- 1 tablespoon lemon juice
- 2 tablespoons extra-virgin olive oil
- 1 cup vegetable broth
- 2 large English cucumbers, peeled and roughly chopped
- 1/2 cup fresh mint leaves
- Salt and pepper to taste

- Optional toppings: diced cucumbers, mint leaves, croutons

Directions:

1. In a blender or food processor, combine the chopped cucumbers, fresh mint leaves, fresh parsley leaves, minced shallot, minced garlic, lemon juice, olive oil, and vegetable broth.
2. Blend on high speed until the mixture becomes smooth and creamy.
3. If the consistency is too thick, you can add more vegetable broth or water to reach your desired texture.
4. Season the gazpacho with salt and pepper to taste. Adjust the seasoning as needed.
5. Transfer the gazpacho to a bowl or large jar and refrigerate for at least 1 hour to chill and allow the flavors to develop.
6. Once chilled, give the gazpacho a good stir before serving.

7. Ladle the Cucumber and Mint Gazpacho into bowls or glasses.
8. If desired, garnish with diced cucumbers, mint leaves, or croutons for added texture and presentation.
9. Serve the gazpacho chilled and savor the refreshing flavors and cooling properties.

Watermelon and Feta Salad with Balsamic Glaze

Ingredients:

- 1 cup crumbled feta cheese
- 1/4 cup fresh mint leaves, torn or chopped
- 1/4 cup sliced red onion
- 1/4 cup toasted pine nuts or chopped walnuts (optional)
- Balsamic glaze, for drizzling
- 4 cups cubed watermelon
- Freshly ground black pepper, to taste

Directions:

1. In a large serving bowl, add the cubed watermelon, crumbled feta cheese, torn or chopped fresh mint leaves, and sliced red onion.

2. Toss gently to combine the Ingredients: and distribute them evenly.
3. If using, sprinkle the toasted pine nuts or chopped walnuts over the salad for added crunch and nuttiness.
4. Drizzle the balsamic glaze generously over the salad.
5. Season with freshly ground black pepper to taste. The saltiness of the feta cheese usually provides enough saltiness to the salad, so additional salt may not be needed.
6. Toss the salad gently again to ensure all the Ingredients:are coated with the balsamic glaze and well combined.
7. Let the salad sit for a few minutes to allow the flavors to meld together.
8. Serve the Watermelon and Feta Salad with Balsamic Glaze immediately, and enjoy the vibrant colors and contrasting flavors.

Broccoli Soup

Ingredients:

- 1 onion, chopped
- 2 cloves of garlic, minced
- 4 cups vegetable broth
- 1 tablespoon olive oil
- 1 teaspoon dried thyme
- 1/2 teaspoon turmeric powder
- Salt and pepper to taste
- 2 heads of broccoli, florets separated
- Fresh lemon juice, for serving
- Optional toppings: sliced almonds, pumpkin seeds, or chopped fresh herbs

Directions:

1. In a large pot, heat the olive oil over medium heat.
2. Add the chopped onion and minced garlic to the pot and sauté until the onion becomes translucent and fragrant.
3. Add the broccoli florets to the pot and sauté for another 2-3 minutes, stirring occasionally.
4. Pour in the vegetable broth, dried thyme, turmeric powder, salt, and pepper. Stir well to combine.
5. Bring the mixture to a boil, then reduce the heat to low and let it simmer for about 15-20 minutes, or until the broccoli is tender.
6. Remove the pot from the heat and allow the soup to cool slightly.
7. Using an immersion blender or a regular blender, puree the soup until smooth and creamy. Be careful when blending hot liquids, as they can create pressure and cause

splatters. If using a regular blender, blend in batches if necessary.
8. Return the soup to the pot and heat it over low heat until warmed through.
9. Taste the soup and adjust the seasoning with salt and pepper if needed.
10. Ladle the Alkaline Broccoli Soup into bowls.
11. Squeeze a bit of fresh lemon juice over each serving to add a hint of brightness.
12. If desired, sprinkle sliced almonds, pumpkin seeds, or chopped fresh herbs on top of the soup for added texture and flavor.
13. Serve the soup hot and enjoy the comforting and alkalizing qualities.

Baked Avocado and Egg

Ingredients:

- 1 ripe avocado
- 2 eggs
- Salt and pepper to taste
- Fresh herbs (e.g., cilantro or parsley), chopped (optional)

Directions:

1. Preheat the oven to 375°F (190°C).
2. Cut the avocado in half and remove the pit.
3. Scoop out a small amount of flesh from each avocado half to create a larger space for the egg.
4. Place the avocado halves in a baking dish.
5. Crack one egg into each avocado half.
6. Season with salt and pepper.

7. Bake for 15-20 minutes or until the egg whites are set.
8. Remove from the oven and sprinkle with fresh herbs if desired.
9. Serve warm.

Overnight Oats

Ingredients:

- 1 tablespoon chia seeds
- 1/2 teaspoon cinnamon
- 1 tablespoon maple syrup
- 1/2 cup rolled oats
- 1/2 cup almond milk (unsweetened)
- 1/4 cup mixed berries

Directions:

1. In a jar or container, combine oats, almond milk, chia seeds, cinnamon, and maple syrup.
2. Stir well, cover, and refrigerate overnight.
3. In the morning, give the mixture a good stir to combine.
4. Top with mixed berries.

5. Enjoy cold or slightly warmed.

Veggie Scramble

Ingredients:

- 1 small zucchini, sliced
- 1 small yellow squash, sliced
- 4 cherry tomatoes, halved
- 4 large eggs
- Salt and pepper to taste
- 1 tablespoon olive oil
- 1/2 red bell pepper, sliced
- 1/2 yellow bell pepper, sliced
- Fresh herbs (e.g., basil or thyme), chopped (optional)

Directions:

1. Heat olive oil in a skillet over medium heat.

2. Add bell peppers, zucchini, and yellow squash.
3. Sauté for 5-7 minutes until slightly softened.
4. Add cherry tomatoes and cook for an additional 2 minutes.
5. In a separate bowl, beat the eggs with salt and pepper.
6. Push the veggies to one side of the skillet and pour the beaten eggs onto the other side.
7. Scramble the eggs until cooked through.
8. Once cooked, mix the eggs with the sautéed vegetables.
9. Remove from heat and sprinkle with fresh herbs if desired.
10. Serve warm.

Oatmeal And Almond Butter

INGREDIENTS:

- 2 cups of oatmeal
- 1 ½ cups of coconut milk
- 1 cup of grated green apple
- 1/3 cup of raw almond butter
- a pinch of cinnamon

DIRECTIONS:

1. Mix the coconut milk, oats and almond butter in a bowl. Add the apple and transfer the mixture to a glass jar.
2. Close with a lid and leave it in the fridge. In the morning, decorate with cinnamon and enjoy.

Bowl With Vegetables

Ingredients:

for the dressing of avocado and cumin

- ¼ teaspoon sea salt

- 2 lemons, freshly squeezed

- 1 cup of filtered water

- 1 tablespoon of extra virgin olive oil

- 1 avocado

- 1 tablespoon cumin powder

- pinch of cayenne pepper

- Optional: ¼ teaspoon smoked paprika

for Tahini lemon dressing:

- 1 clove of chopped garlic

- 1 tablespoon of extra virgin olive oil
- ¾ teaspoon sea salt
- Black pepper to taste
- ¼ cup of tahini
- ½ lemon, freshly squeezed
- ½ cup of filtered water

for the salad:

- 3 cups kale, chopped
- ½ cup of broccoli florets, chopped
- 1/3 cup of cherry tomatoes, cut in half
- ½ zucchini, spiralized
- ½ cup of kelp noodles, soaked and drained
- 2 tablespoons of hemp seeds

DIRECTIONS:

1. Steam the broccoli and kale and set aside. Then, mix the seaweed noodles and the zucchini noodles, and pour a generous serving of smoked avocado cumin dressing.
2. Add some cherry tomatoes. Mix once more, and then steamed vegetables. Sprinkle with lemon tahini dressing, and then add tomatoes and noodles on top. Sprinkle with hemp seeds.

Zucchini Noodles And Kale Pesto

INGREDIENTS:

- 2 freshly squeezed lemons
- 1 bunch of kale
- 2 cups fresh basil
- 1/4 cup extra virgin olive oil
- 1 zucchini noodles (spiral)
- 1/2 cup of nuts
- Sea salt and pepper
- Optional: sliced asparagus, spinach leaves and tomato

DIRECTIONS:

1. Soak the nuts the night before.The next morning, mix all the Ingredients:in a blender

until you get a smooth mixture, and simply add the zucchini noodles.

Crunchy Kale Salad with Tahini Dressing

Ingredients:

SALAD

- Carrot, organic, one shredded

- Radishes, organic, thin sliced

- Brussel sprouts, organic, eight, sliced thin

- Kale, organic, chopped with stalks removed, four cups

- Basil, chopped, one cup

- Pumpkin seeds, one tablespoon

- Cashews, one tablespoon

- Almonds, chopped, two tablespoons

- Cannellini beans, .5 cup

TAHINI DRESSING

- Flax oil, one tablespoon

- Garlic, organic, one clove minced

- Tahini, one tablespoon

- Sea salt, .5 teaspoon

- Black pepper, one teaspoon

- Lemon juice, organic, two tablespoons

- Avocado, organic, one half

Directions:
1. To make the dressing mix together all of the Ingredients: listed for the dressing until the mix is smooth.
2. Mix all of the salad Ingredients: and pour the dressing over the salad.

Raw Pad Thai with Zucchini Noodles

Ingredients:

PAD THAI

- Sprouts, organic, one cup washed and dried

- Red cabbage, organic, one cup shredded

- Green onions, organic, two chopped

- Carrots, organic, three large

- Zucchini, organic, three medium sized

- Coconut oil, two tablespoons

- Cilantro, organic, one bunch chopped

- Cauliflower florets, organic, one cup

SAUCE

- Ginger root, organic, one inch grated

- Garlic, organic, one clove minced

- Lime juice, organic, two tablespoons

- Honey, raw organic, one tablespoon

- Tamari, .25 cup

- Almond butter, .25 cup

- Tahini, .25 cup

Directions:

1. Make noodles from the zucchini and the carrot by either using a mandolin or a spiralizer.
2. A vegetable peeler also works well to make long thin strips.
3. Add these to a bowl with the cilantro, cauliflower, sprouts, cabbage, and onions. Blend together the ginger, garlic, lime juice, honey, tamari, tahini, and almond butter.

4. This sauce is supposed to be very thick but if it feels too thick to work with add a few drops of water until the consistency is easier to stir.
5. Pour the sauce into the vegetables and mix well to coat all vegetables with the sauce.

Chickpea Quinoa Vegetable Bowl

Ingredients:

BOWL

- Kale, organic, one bunch remove stalks and slice leaves thin

- Chickpeas, organic, one cup cooked drained rinsed

- Cauliflower, organic, broken into florets, one cup

- Celery, organic, three stalks sliced thin

- Carrots, organic, peel and slice thin

- Red onion, organic, slice thin

- Olive oil, three tablespoons

- Quinoa, two cups cooked

- Sea salt, one teaspoon

- Black pepper, two teaspoons

- Parsley, organic, fresh, .5 cup chopped

- Pecans, organic, toasted, .25 cup chopped

- Apricots, organic, dried, .25 cup chopped

- Cherry tomatoes, organic, one cup sliced in half

- Baby spinach, organic, two cups

DRESSING

- Dijon mustard, one teaspoon

- Honey, raw organic, one teaspoon

- Lemon juice, organic, two tablespoons

- Olive oil, .25 cup

- Red pepper flakes, .25 teaspoon

- Ginger, organic, one one-half inch piece peel and mince

Directions:

1. Divide the warm cooked quinoa into two bowls. Cook the celery, carrots, and onion in oil for five minutes.
2. Stir in the chickpeas, kale, and cauliflower and cook five minutes stirring often.
3. Add in the tomatoes and spinach, stirring while the spinach wilts, about three minutes.
4. Pour this mix over the quinoa and top with the dried apricots. Add on the mixed dressing to taste.

CANNELLINI BEAN & ARTICHOKE SPREAD

Ingredients:

- 2/3 cup of olive oil

- 2 tins of cannellini beans, drained and rinsed - organic if possible

- 2 tins of artichoke bottoms or artichoke hearts and drained-organic

- 1/2 teaspoon of sea salt

- 1/2 teaspoon of fresh ground pepper

- 2 garlic cloves roughly chopped

- 2 shallot roughly chopped

- 4 tablespoons lemon juice

- 2 teaspoons lemon zest

- 20-24 tarragon leaves

Directions:
1. You place all these Ingredients:in a food processor with the s blade
2. You pulse to combine
3. You turn off processor
4. You scrape down sides of a bowl
5. You blend again until they are combined
6. You add additional oil to make a spreadable consistency
7. You season to taste with the extra salt

HEARTY VEGETABLE SOUP

Ingredients:

- 1/2 red pepper, seeded & diced

- 1/2 jar of cannellini beans, rinsed

- 1/4 cup of fresh chopped parsley, additional 1 tbsp for garnish

- Sea salt or Himalayan salt

- 1/4 cup of fresh chopped parsley, additional 1 tbsp for garnish

- Additional Veggies Required (Broth)

- 1/8 onion

- 1/8 small cabbage

- 1 small zucchini

- 2 carrots
- 2 ribs celery
- 1/4 red pepper
- 1/2 onion, diced
- 1 clove garlic, crushed or minced
- 1 1/2 large carrots, diced
- 1 1/2 potatoes, diced
- 1/2 cup of the diced autumn squash
- 1 large tomato, diced
- 2 ribs celery, diced
- 1 small zucchini, diced
- Filtered water

Directions:

1. You run all broth veggies through a juicer
2. Then, you set aside
3. You add diced onion and garlic with 1 to 2 tbsp of filtered water in a large pot
4. You steam fry for some minutes until you see onions are translucent
5. You add broth & 1 cup filtered water
6. You heat broth
7. You add carrots, potatoes and squash
8. You simmer for 5 minutes
9. You add celery & zucchini
10. You simmer for 5 minutes
11. You add peppers, tomatoes and cannellini beans
12. You simmer for five more minutes
13. You add a little amount of water about ½ cup if you see broth seems too little
14. You test for flavor
15. You season with sea salt or Himalayan salt
16. You stir in chopped herbs

17. You ladle into some bowls
18. You garnish with the fresh chopped basil & parsley
19. You sprinkled with the hemp nuts for a good protein measure

SESAME TAHINI DRESSING

Ingredients:

- 2 avocado
- 1 cup raw sesame tahini
- 1 cup extra virgin olive oil
- Juice of 2 – 3 lemons

Directions:
1. You place all these ingredients in a blender or food processor
2. You blend/process until smooth and creamy

Cucumber-Mint Infused Water

Ingredients:

- 1 cucumber, sliced
- Fresh mint leaves
- Water

Directions:

1. Fill a pitcher or large jar with water.
2. Add the sliced cucumber and a handful of fresh mint leaves.
3. Stir gently to mix the Ingredients:.
4. Place the pitcher in the refrigerator and let it sit for at least 1 hour to allow the flavors to infuse.
5. Serve the cucumber-mint infused water over ice for a refreshing and hydrating alkaline beverage.

Green Detox Smoothie

Ingredients:

- 1/2 lemon, juiced
- 1/2 cup coconut water
- Ice cubes (optional)
- 1 cup spinach
- 1/2 cucumber, chopped
- 1 celery stalk, chopped
- 1 green apple, cored and chopped

Directions:
1. Place all the Ingredients: in a blender.
2. Blend until smooth and well combined.
3. If desired, add ice cubes and blend again for a chilled smoothie.

4. Pour the green detox smoothie into a glass and enjoy as a refreshing alkaline beverage packed with nutrients.

Yummy Cold Oats

Ingredients:

- 1/2 cup yogurt
- 1/2 teaspoon cinnamon
- 1/2 sliced banana
- 1/2 teaspoon peanut butter
- 1/2 cup oats
- 1/2 cup of skimmed milk
- 1/2 cup of berries

Directions:

1. Combine the oats, yogurt, milk, and salt in a bowl. Pour the mixture into a glass jar.
2. Refrigerate the jar overnight after sealing it.
3. In the morning, add sliced bananas, berries, and cinnamon.

Scrambled Tofu

Ingredients:

- 1/2 teaspoons of paprika
- 1/2 teaspoons of turmeric
- 1/2 cup of yeast
- 1/2 cups of baby spinach
- 100g tofu
- I onion
- 3 cloves
- 3 tomatoes
- 1/2 teaspoons of cumin
- Add salt to taste

Directions:

1. Chop the garlic and dice the onion.
2. Add onions to a heated pan and cook for 7 minutes.
3. Cook the garlic for one minute.
4. Include tofu and tomatoes. Continue cooking for ten minutes.
5. Add water, cumin, and paprika. Stir thoroughly and cook.
6. The spinach should be the last to add.

Thewlis

Ingredients:

- 1/2 cups chickpea flour
- Add salt to taste.
- A pinch of turmeric
- Water is used to knead the dough.
- 2 teaspoons of olive oil for the dough
- 1/2 cup fenugreek leaves
- 1 clove of garlic that has been chopped
- 1/2 cups of spinach
- 1 1/2 cups of either oat flour or wheat flour
- 4 tablespoons of olive oil will be used for the cooking.

Directions:

1. Combine the flours, fenugreek leaves, turmeric, salt, and water.
2. Heat some oil in a pan for two minutes.
3. Add the onions and stir until the mixture turns golden.
4. Add spinach and simmer for two minutes. Take it off the heat source and allow it to cool.
5. Add the prepared spinach to the dough and thoroughly knead it.
6. Separate the dough into tiny balls. Roll the dough into small circles using a rolling pin.
7. Cook the thepla for two minutes on each side in a heated skillet.
8. Cook for ten seconds on each side after adding one teaspoon of oil and cooking for the full minute. Serve hot!

Guacamole with Veggie Sticks

Ingredients:

- ½ cup chopped cherry tomatoes
- ¼ cup chopped red onion
- Juice of 1 lime
- 2 tablespoons chopped fresh cilantro
- Salt and pepper to taste
- 2 ripe avocados
- ½ cup chopped cucumber
- 12 cup chopped, any-color bell peppers

For the veggie sticks:

- Carrot sticks
- Celery sticks

- Cucumber sticks

- Bell pepper sticks (any color)

Directions:

1. Remove the pit from the avocados before cutting them in half lengthwise. Scoop out the flesh into a bowl and mash with a fork until desired consistency.
2. Add the chopped cucumber, bell peppers, cherry tomatoes, red onion, lime juice, and cilantro to the mashed avocado. Mix well.
3. Season with salt and pepper to taste.
4. Serve the guacamole with carrot sticks, celery sticks, cucumber sticks, and bell pepper sticks.

Arugula, Beetroot, and Walnut Salad

Ingredients:

- 1/2 cup walnuts, roughly chopped
- 1/4 cup crumbled goat cheese or feta cheese (optional)
- 2 tablespoons balsamic vinegar
- 2 tablespoons extra-virgin olive oil
- 4 cups arugula leaves
- 2 medium-sized beetroots, roasted and sliced
- Salt and pepper to taste

Directions:
1. In a large salad bowl, add the arugula leaves.
2. Place the roasted beetroots on a cutting board and slice them into thin rounds or wedges.

3. Add the sliced beetroots to the salad bowl with the arugula.
4. Sprinkle the chopped walnuts and crumbled goat cheese or feta cheese (if using) over the salad.
5. In a small bowl, whisk together the balsamic vinegar, extra-virgin olive oil, salt, and pepper to make the dressing.
6. Drizzle the dressing over the salad, and toss gently to coat the Ingredients:evenly.
7. Adjust the seasoning if needed.
8. Let the salad sit for a few minutes to allow the flavors to meld together.
9. Serve the Arugula, Beetroot, and Walnut Salad as a refreshing side dish or a light meal.

Cauliflower and Coconut Curry Soup

Ingredients:

- 1 tablespoon curry powder

- 1 teaspoon ground turmeric

- 1 can (13.5 oz) coconut milk

- 4 cups vegetable broth

- 2 tablespoons coconut oil or olive oil

- Salt and pepper to taste

- Fresh cilantro leaves, for garnish (optional)

- 1 medium-sized cauliflower, florets separated

- 1 onion, chopped

- 3 cloves of garlic, minced

- Squeeze of fresh lime or lemon juice (optional)

Directions:

1. In a large pot, heat the coconut oil or olive oil over medium heat.
2. Add the chopped onion to the pot and sauté until it becomes translucent and fragrant.
3. Add the minced garlic, curry powder, and ground turmeric to the pot. Stir well to coat the onions with the spices and cook for about 1 minute, until fragrant.
4. Add the cauliflower florets to the pot and stir to combine with the onion and spice mixture.
5. Pour in the vegetable broth and bring the mixture to a boil.
6. Reduce the heat to low, cover the pot, and simmer for about 15-20 minutes, or until the cauliflower is tender.
7. Remove the pot from the heat and allow the soup to cool slightly.

8. Using an immersion blender or a regular blender, puree the soup until smooth and creamy. Be cautious when blending hot liquids, as they can create pressure and cause splatters. If using a regular blender, blend in batches if necessary.
9. Return the soup to the pot and place it back on low heat.
10. Stir in the coconut milk and simmer for an additional 5 minutes, allowing the flavors to meld together.
11. Season the soup with salt and pepper to taste. Adjust the seasoning as needed.
12. Ladle the Cauliflower and Coconut Curry Soup into bowls.
13. Garnish with fresh cilantro leaves, if desired, and squeeze a bit of fresh lime or lemon juice over each serving for a tangy kick.
14. Serve the soup hot and savor the creamy, flavorful, and aromatic qualities.

Quinoa Salad

Ingredients:

- 2 tablespoons fresh lemon juice
- 2 tablespoons extra-virgin olive oil
- 2 tablespoons chopped fresh parsley
- 1 tablespoon chopped fresh mint
- 1 cup cooked quinoa
- 1 cup cherry tomatoes, halved
- 1 cucumber, diced
- 1 bell pepper, diced (red, yellow, or orange)
- 1/2 red onion, thinly sliced
- 1/4 cup Kalamata olives, pitted and halved
- 1/4 cup crumbled feta cheese (optional)

- Salt and pepper to taste

Directions:

1. In a large salad bowl, combine the cooked quinoa, cherry tomatoes, diced cucumber, diced bell pepper, thinly sliced red onion, and halved Kalamata olives.
2. If using, sprinkle the crumbled feta cheese over the salad.
3. In a small bowl, whisk together the fresh lemon juice, extra-virgin olive oil, chopped fresh parsley, chopped fresh mint, salt, and pepper to make the dressing.
4. Drizzle the dressing over the salad and toss gently to coat all the Ingredients:evenly.
5. Taste the salad and adjust the seasoning with salt and pepper if needed.
6. Let the Mediterranean Quinoa Salad sit for a few minutes to allow the flavors to meld together.

7. Serve the salad at room temperature or chilled.

Almond Butter and Banana Toast

Ingredients:

- 2 tablespoons almond butter

- 1 ripe banana, sliced

- 1 tablespoon hemp seeds (optional)

- 2 slices whole-grain bread (gluten-free if desired)

- 1 teaspoon honey or maple syrup (optional)

Directions:

1. Toast the bread slices until golden brown.
2. Spread almond butter evenly over each slice.
3. Arrange banana slices on top of one slice.
4. Sprinkle with hemp seeds if desired.
5. Drizzle with honey or maple syrup if desired.
6. Place the other slice of bread on top to form a sandwich.

7. Cut in half if desired and serve.

Acai Bowl

Ingredients:

- 1/2 cup almond milk (unsweetened)
- 1/4 cup fresh or frozen berries (e.g., blueberries, strawberries)
- 1/4 cup granola
- 1 tablespoon unsweetened coconut flakes
- 1 tablespoon chia seeds (optional)
- 1 frozen acai packet
- 1 ripe banana, frozen
- 1 tablespoon nut butter (such as almond or cashew butter)

Directions:

1. In a blender, combine frozen acai, frozen banana, almond milk, and berries.

2. Blend until smooth and creamy.
3. Pour the mixture into a bowl.
4. Top with granola, coconut flakes, chia seeds, and a drizzle of nut butter.
5. Serve immediately.

Chickpea Omelets

Ingredients:

- 1/2 teaspoon turmeric powder
- 1/2 teaspoon cumin powder
- Salt and pepper to taste
- 1 tablespoon olive oil
- 1/2 red onion, sliced
- 1/2 bell pepper, diced
- Handful of spinach leaves
- 1/4 cup sliced cherry tomatoes
- 1 cup chickpea flour
- 1 cup water
- 1 teaspoon nutritional yeast

- Fresh herbs (e.g., parsley or basil), chopped (optional)

Directions:

1. In a bowl, whisk together chickpea flour, water, nutritional yeast, turmeric powder, cumin powder, salt, and pepper until well combined.
2. Heat olive oil in a non-stick skillet over medium heat.
3. Add onion, bell pepper, and spinach leaves. Sauté for 3-4 minutes until slightly softened.
4. Pour half of the chickpea batter into the skillet and spread evenly to cover the vegetables.
5. Cook for 3-4 minutes until the bottom is golden brown and the edges start to crisp up.
6. Flip the omelets carefully using a spatula and cook for an additional 3-4 minutes.
7. Transfer the omelets to a plate and repeat with the remaining batter.

8. Once cooked, top with sliced cherry tomatoes and fresh herbs if desired.
9. Serve warm.

Energy Shake

INGREDIENTS:

- 2 cups of homemade almond milk
- 1 frozen banana
- 1 tablespoon of coconut oil
- 2 cups fresh spinach
- 1 cup of frozen mixed berries
- 2 tablespoons of raw almond butter
- ½ teaspoon of cinnamon

DIRECTIONS:

1. In a blender, mix the almond milk and spinach, and then add the other ingredients. Mix once more and enjoy it.

Quinoa Burrito Bowl

INGREDIENTS:

- 4 cloves of garlic, chopped.

- 2 limes, fresh juice.

- 2 avocados, sliced.

- 1 spoonful of cumin.

- 1 cup of quinoa

- 4 sliced green onions

- 2 cans of black beans or adzuki.

- A small handful of coriander, chopped.

DIRECTIONS:

1. Cook the quinoa, and in a large skillet, heat the beans over low heat.

2. Add the lime juice, cumin, garlic and onion, and cook for 10 to 15 minutes. Add fresh cilantro and avocado on top.

Wild Rice Mushrooms And Almond Risotto

INGREDIENTS:

- 1 tablespoon of extra virgin olive oil

- ½ cup of raw walnut halves

- cups chopped celery

- ½ of yellow onion; cut

- 4 medium white whole mushrooms; sliced

- 2 cloves of garlic, chopped

- cups uncooked brown rice

- 2 cups of vegetable broth

- ½ cup sliced green onions

- Salt and pepper to taste

DIRECTIONS:

1. In a medium skillet, sauté the mushrooms, onion, garlic and a cup of celery, stir and cook until the celery and onion are tender. Add the broth and brown rice, and boil.
2. Lower the heat, simmer, cover the pan and cook for an hour. Stir for 30 minutes. Remove the rice from the heat when finished, remove the lid and add the green onions, and ½ cup of chopped celery.
3. Next, set the oven to 180 ° C and line a baking sheet with parchment paper. Then, spread the nuts and toast for 8-10 minutes, turning them in half. When finished, cut the pecans and add them to the risotto.

Eggplant Chickpea Stew

Ingredients:

- Chickpeas, organic, one cup
- Cilantro, organic, three tablespoons for garnish
- Eggplant, organic, one cut into cubes
- Yellow onion, organic, one diced small
- Tomato puree, organic, one cup
- Chili powder, one tablespoon
- Olive oil, two tablespoons
- Millet, one cup cooked
- Black pepper, one teaspoon
- Sea salt, one teaspoon

- Garlic, organic, three cloves minced

Directions:
1. Cook eggplant, salt, pepper, garlic, and onion with oil for fifteen minutes.
2. Add in the tomatoes, chili powder, and chickpeas and cook another ten minutes. Pour this mixture over the hot millet to serve.

CUCUMBER & TOMATILLO BREAKFAST SHAKE

Ingredients:

- 4 scoops of Super Soy Sprouts
- 2 scoops of Super Greens
- 1 cup of water
- 1 cup of Rice Dream
- 2 unpeeled, unwaxed cucumber
- 2 tomatillos
- 4 cups of organic baby spinach juice of 1 lime
- 12 to16 ice cubes

Directions:
1. You slice vegetables
2. You put all these ingredients a few at a time into a blender

3. You blend until smooth
4. You add ice cubes last

BLACK BEAN & TOMATO SOUP

Ingredients:

- 2 clove garlic, chopped

- Sea salt to taste

- 2 medium carrots, diced

- 2 bay leaves

- 1 tsp. of oregano

- 1 tsp. of cayenne pepper

- 2 lb. of dry beans rinsed well

- 6-8 tomatoes, diced

- 2 medium onions, chopped

- 1/2 cup of olive oil

- 1/2 cup of fresh cilantro

Directions:

1. You cook beans until tender
2. You warm olive oil (not hot)
3. You add seasoning
4. You continue warming oil
5. You stir continuously to release flavors
6. You combine all ingredients in a pan
7. You add water to reach desired consistency
8. You heat to just before a boil
9. You need to be sure not to boil the soup

RAW CHOCOLATE PUDDING

Ingredients:

- 1/2 tsp of pure alcohol free vanilla,

- 6 drops of liquid stevia

- 3 tsp of agave syrup

- 1 pinch of celtic sea salt

- 15 tbsp of almond milk

- 3 medium sized avocados

- 2 heaping tbsp of hemp nuts

- 4 tbsp of raw cacao powder

- Cacao nibs

Directions:

1. You place all these ingredients into your blender
2. You combine until you see it is creamy & silky smooth
3. You add some extra tablespoons of the almond milk to create a consistency
4. You spoon into the serving dish
5. You sprinkle top with some cacao nibs and enjoy

Maple Millet Porridge

Ingredients:

- 1 cup of millet
- 4 cups of water
- A pinch of salt
- 1 teaspoon of cinnamon
- Depending on personal preference, maple syrup

Directions:
1. In a big pot, bring the water to a boil.
2. Add the millet and salt to the pan.
3. Cover and reduce the heat. Cook for around 15 minutes.
4. Combine cinnamon with almond water.
5. Cook the millets for an additional 20 minutes.

6. Add maple syrup and mix well. Consider adjusting the thickness.
7. Your meal is now served!

Chickpea Fritatta

Ingredients:

- 1/2 teaspoon black pepper
- 4 tablespoons of olive oil
- 1 clove of garlic that is grated
- 1/2 cups chopped spring onions
- 1 cup chickpea flour
- 1 cup of water
- 1 cup of sliced zucchini
- 1/2 cups chopped onion
- Season with salt to taste.

Directions:

1. Preheat the oven to 375 degrees Fahrenheit (190 degrees Celsius).
2. Grease a pan or tray for baking.
3. Add all Ingredients:except the oil and spring onions to a large basin.
4. Add 1-2 tablespoons of oil to the batter in the large bowl.
5. Add it to the pan or tray that has been greased.
6. Cook for 30 to 45 minutes.
7. Remove the meat and cut it into pieces.
8. Serve garnished with spring onions.

Alkaline Berry Crumble

Ingredients:

- one cup of rolled oats //

- 1/4 cup melted coconut oil

- One-fourth cup of almond butter

- One-fourth cup of maple syrup

- 1 teaspoon cinnamon, ground

- 1 tablespoon of lemon juice and 2 cups of mixed berries, including strawberries, blueberries, and raspberries.

- One spoonful of maple syrup.

- One cup of almond flour

- A dash of salt

Directions:

1. The oven should be preheated at 350°F (175°C). Using coconut oil or parchment paper, grease or line a baking pan.
2. Combine the mixed berries, 1 tablespoon of maple syrup, and lemon juice in a bowl. Toss the berries carefully to coat them. Add the fruit mixture to the baking dish.
3. Combine the almond butter, melted coconut oil, rolled oats, maple syrup, cinnamon, and sea salt in a separate bowl. Mix thoroughly until a crumble-like consistency emerges.
4. Evenly cover the berries in the baking dish with the crumble mixture.
5. Bake for 30-35 minutes, or until the crumble topping is golden and the berries are bubbling.
6. Take the dish out of the oven and allow it cool before serving. Serve warm as is or with a

drizzle of almond milk or a dollop of coconut yogurt for richness.

www.ingramcontent.com/pod-product-compliance
Lightning Source LLC
LaVergne TN
LVHW010220070526
838199LV00062B/4675